"Did I Tell You About When Your Parents Were Children?"

Deborah Shaw Lewis and Gregg Lewis

ZondervanPublishingHouse
Grand Rapids, Michigan

A Division of HarperCollins*Publishers*

"Did I Ever Tell You About When Your Parents Were Children?"
Copyright © 1994 by Deborah Shaw Lewis and Gregg Lewis

Zondervan Publishing House
Grand Rapids, Michigan 49530

Library of Congress Cataloging-in-Publication Data

Lewis, Deborah Shaw, 1951–
      "Did I ever tell you about when your parents were children?" : building
togetherness and values by sharing stories about your family / by Deborah Shaw
Lewis and Gregg Lewis.
      p. cm. — (Family share together)
      ISBN 0-310-42101-2 (pbk.)
      1. Family—Anecdotes. 2. Parents—Anecdotes. 3. Storytelling. 4. Family—Folklore.
5. Oral biography. I. Lewis, Gregg A. II. Title. III. Series: Lewis, Deborah Shaw, 1951–
Family share-together book.
HQ518.L4823   1994   94-30744
306.85—dc20   CIP

Illustrations by Liz Conrad

Printed in the United States of America

94 95 96 97 98 99 / ❖ CH / 6 5 4 3 2 1

Welcome to the Adventure of Storytelling!

Susan greeted her visitor warmly. Laura was the eighteen-year-old daughter of two old college friends whom Susan had seen only periodically over the years. Laura's parents had let Susan know that Laura was going through a time of teenage rebellion and that only under severe parental pressure had she enrolled at the Christian college where Susan taught. Susan felt pretty sure that Laura hadn't really wanted to accept her invitation to visit.

"You know, during our college days together, I was student-body vice-president while your father was student-body president," Susan commented, trying to break the ice.

"My dad? Student-body president? You've *got* to be kidding!"

Susan laughed at Laura's obvious surprise. "No kidding. Your father was the big man on campus. When your parents began going together, your mother was the envy of half the girls in school. But then your mom was pretty popular herself. You might say they were *the* campus couple."

"Really?" Laura looked incredulous.

Susan spent the rest of the afternoon telling about shared collegiate adventures and misadventures. Each story was news to Laura, who had no concept of her parents being gifted, fun-loving, or occasionally mischievous. She saw them as only strict and demanding parents.

Laura left Susan's home with a new understanding of her parents. It probably would have done Laura's parents some good to have heard those stories again, too.

Our own family's adventure in storytelling began one weekend several years ago on our way back from a weekend visit to Grandpa Lewis. I had wanted Grandpa Lewis, who was such a good storyteller, to tell the story of "The Voice in the Barn." I knew that at age ninety he would not have much longer to tell it, so on our last morning there, I gathered my children and asked Grandpa to tell the story. I was so disappointed! Grandpa had hardly started when he began to ramble, confusing details and going off on tangents. Even Gregg and I could hardly follow the plotline.

On the way home, I tried to explain what Grandpa had been trying to say, and as I explained, I began to tell the story as I remembered it. Gregg broke in occasionally to add details. Our children sat spellbound as we stumbled through the story, and when we finished, they begged, "Tell us another one!"

So I dug through my memory and told them the story of the day my family had been on vacation in Kentucky and I got left behind at a gas station. Gregg told the story of his first day of school, when he ran and hid between pews in the church near the bus stop. After that I told a story my mother had told me about how I almost died of pneumonia when I was two months old. Between us, Gregg and I told some stories we'd heard from our grandparents, others our parents had told, and quite a few from our own childhood memories. The kids loved them.

That trip home was such fun! Telling stories that day filled a need in me, in Gregg, and apparently in our children.

Thus began our family story times. Family storytelling became an exciting adventure, and we discovered our own unique heritage through storytelling. We hope you will, too.

Maybe you are thinking, "I'm no storyteller! Nothing interesting ever happens to me!"

Then keep reading! For the rest of this book will be especially helpful for anyone who feels he or she has no story to tell. While it may be true that many of us will never be great storytellers, everyone has stories worth telling. We need only to search our minds and memories to uncover a whole repertoire of potential stories.

It may help to think of the human memory as a computer. To call up information from our mind, we must first find the right file and a key word to access that file.

Or, we can think of our memories as a sprawling house, built by a creative contractor who simply added rooms hither and yon as they were needed. Rediscovering memories is like walking down the twisting, turning hallways of that home and seeing closed doors in every direction.

In the pages that follow, our "Story Starters" and "Storytelling Tips" include a hodgepodge, bushel-basket full of story-related questions, suggestions, and comments to consider. You might want to think of them as a computer menu for calling up the files of your memory. Or as a set of keys for you to use to unlock the doors of your own rambling house of recollections.

You can use the "Story Starters" and "Storytelling Tips" as a personal checklist to get you thinking of stories to tell your children. Or at your next family gathering, you could ask some of these questions to your siblings or older family members, and let them help you come up with stories to tell.

Some entries on a computer menu are seldom used. A few keys on our old key rings no longer open any doors. In the same way, not all of the following questions will effectively trigger your memories or elicit forgotten experiences. But some of them will. And when they do, there you will find a starting place for your own adventure of family storytelling.

*Tell about one of your
early memories of your
mother or father.*

- What did your parents look like?
- Describe the sound of their voices.
- What times during the day did you enjoy being with your father or your mother?
- What traditions or routines do you associate with them?
- What did they do for a living?
- What favorite foods did your mother cook?
- Did your father ever cook the meals?

As you are telling your children about the people of your past, especially your parents and siblings, fill in the important details. Make sure your children know names and ages. For example: "I was seven years old at the time, so my brother Terrell would have been eleven. You know, he is four years older than I am, just like Andrew is four years older than Lisette." Details not only add to the story but also give a frame of reference.

Tell about a day,
as a child,
when you were afraid.

- Describe the events that led up to your fear.
- Who was with you that day?
- What did you do?
- Who comforted you?

When Gregg or I tell a story about our childhoods, we give our children a new view of us—that we were once children who were sometimes mischievous, sometimes afraid, sometimes funny, sometimes lonely. As they identify with us, they also realize that they, too, can triumph over their troubles or fears and become adults. Each family story adds to our family's sense of identity and connects us in a deeper way. Our telling family stories enables our children to glimpse both the past and the future.

*Tell about a day,
as a child,
when you were angry.*

- What happened to make you angry?
- Who else was involved?
- How was the issue resolved?
- Now tell about a time when you were lonely, shy, embarrassed, or sad.

Before our culture became so mobile and families so distanced from one another, children learned life's important lessons from the stories told at home of how their parents grew up, conquered problems, resolved conflicts, and moved to new places. When we tell family stories, we communicate with the next generation. Stories are a good place to express feelings, to share or test ideas, to gain new knowledge, and to pass on values.

Which chore did you hate to do when you were a child?

- How old were you when your parents began to have you help around the house?
- What was your first job?
- Tell your children about the time you refused to do your chores.
- What chores did your brothers or sisters do?
- Did you ever wish you had one of their jobs?

Stories I tell fall into three categories. First are full-blown stories that I have thought through, prepared, and dramatized (see pages 20–25). These I tell over and over. Then I stumble through on-the-spot stories when a specific incident triggers a memory (see pages 38–40). Sometimes these develop into full-blown stories. The third type I call "grits" stories. These are a collection of interesting facts, thoughts, and memories about a subject (see pages 72–74).

*Did you ever lose something
that was very important to you,
or break something
that couldn't be fixed?*

A way to add interest to stories is to add dramatic emphasis. When I tell about the time I jumped out my bedroom window, I exclaim, "Whoo—ee! That was fun!" Or I tell of being excited and my heart's going "thumpity-thump-thump" as I beat out that rhythm on my chest. Sometimes you will want to use different voices for different people in your story. I drop my voice to a deeper tone to imitate my father. I use a higher pitch to be a child.

*Tell about a time
when you deliberately
disobeyed your mother
or your father.*

- What were you thinking at the time?
- How old were you?
- In which house were you living?
- How were you found out?
- How were you disciplined?
- What did you learn from the experience?

One of my children's favorite stories is that of my only belt spanking (see the following page). I had been disobedient and hid. My children laugh; but they also understand, without my quoting a single Bible verse, that all have sinned—even their mother. They also see my father's love for me and begin to understand that discipline is a reflection of love.

My One and Only Belt Spanking

This story is one of my children's favorites. This is a full-blown story. I have thought it through, prepared it, and dramatized it. And I have told it over and over for a variety of audiences.

On the day I am going to tell you about, I was either eight or nine years old. And while I am not sure how old I was, I am sure of one thing: I was old enough to know better!

I don't know what gave me the idea—maybe I saw Superman or Batman on television—but I decided to jump out of my bedroom window. Now, my bedroom was on the end of the house where the basement was partly above ground. So it wasn't like jumping out a second-story window, where I would surely have been hurt. It wasn't like climbing out a ground-floor window either. It was high enough off the ground that I could have hurt myself.

And that is just . . . what I was thinking . . . as I squatted on the windowsill and looked down. *(I peer down at my toes.)* Whew! It was a far piece down!

But I had made up my mind to do this, so I got up my courage and I . . . jumped! *(I jump in place.)*

Whoo—ee! That was fun! Boy, it was fun! . . . until . . . I looked up and saw Daddy coming at me across the yard. *(I point over in the distance.)* He had seen me jump! I could tell by the look on his face . . . he was not a happy man.

"Deborah Ruth Shaw *(I say in a deep voice)*, you could have broken your leg! Don't you *ever* jump out that window again."

"Yes, Daddy." *(I say in a high-pitched voice.)* "I won't do it again, Daddy."

And Daddy smiled at me and tousled my hair. *(I reach over and tousle the hair of a child close to me.)* He went back to whatever he had been doing on the other side of the yard.

Now, my mouth may have been saying, "Yes, Daddy. I won't do it again, Daddy." But my heart was going thumpity-thump-thump *(I pat my hand against my chest and beat out that rhythm)*, and I was remembering . . . how much fun it had been.

So, do you know what I did? I walked right back in that house, *(here I pick up the pace)* through the breezeway, into the kitchen, down the hall, past the den, past the bathroom, into my bedroom, climbed into the window, and looked down. Whew! It was a far piece down!

But I remembered how much fun it had been . . . and I got my courage up . . . and . . . I . . . jumped! Whoo—ee, it was *fun!*

Until . . . I looked up and saw my daddy *(again I point)* coming across that yard again. That man had a thunderstorm on his face!

In that instant, looking at Daddy's face, I made . . . the worst decision . . . I could possibly have made. I decided to run!

And I ran *(I pick up the pace, running in place)* into the house, through the breezeway, into the kitchen, and down the hall. I looked into the den and thought, *Oh, no, my daddy will find me in the den.* So I ran all the way down the hall to my bedroom and looked in there. *Oh, no!* I thought, *My daddy will surely look in my room.* So I ran back up the hall, into the bathroom, and wiggled down between . . . the toilet . . . and . . . the wall.

And I hoped that my daddy wouldn't find me. But he did.

He pulled me out from between the toilet and the wall. "Deborah Ruth Shaw," *(in a deep voice)* "I told you not to jump out that window again!"

"I know, Daddy." *(High-pitched voice again.)* "I'm *sorry*, Daddy!"

Then, to my horror *(each word spoken separately and slowly)*, he began to unbuckle his belt. I was going to get . . . a belt spanking! *(I pick up the pace a little.)* I had never had a belt spanking before! I had seen my brother Terry get a belt spanking, and I just *knew* that they were awful!

Now, if I had been facing my mother, she would have sent me to get a switch (she was big on switching). With my mother you had to be very, *very* careful to get the right switch. If you didn't she would look at the switch critically and say, "Deborah Ruth Shaw, this is too small, go get me another one." Or it would be too big or too short or too something.

I don't remember any of my mother's switchings being painful. But I have a vivid memory of the agony of standing in front of the bushes on the side of the yard, shifting from one foot to the other, trying to pick the right switch. *Oh, if I pick this one, it won't hurt so much. But Mama will probably send me back for a bigger one. And if I pick this bigger one, oh-h-h, it will hurt!*

No matter how long I agonized over a switch, no matter how careful I was, I *never* picked a good switch the first time. And if I had done something particularly mischievous, my mama would even send me a third time.

I was a grown woman . . . with children of my own . . . before I realized that the picking of the switch had been the *main* part of my punishment.

But on this particular occasion, I was *not* facing my mother. I was facing my father. And *(slow pace)* he was pulling his belt off, oh-so-slowly. He doubled it over. He made me lean over his knee. And *pop! (I clap my hands loudly.)* He popped me once with that belt. And oh! It hurt! *(Long pause, then a loud sigh.)* But, I never, *ever* jumped out that window again.

*Tell about the park
near your house
where you liked to play.*

- What was your favorite piece of playground equipment?
- What happened there?
- Tell a story about games you liked to play.

Different children have different listening skills. Be willing to vary how much detail you include, how much emphasis you put on the action, and how long you talk. A story for young children should be simple and direct, with events in chronological order and an emphasis on action. As children get older and become more experienced listeners, they will listen to longer, more detailed stories, with more description and less action. They will listen to stories with smaller stories inside, or several stories strung together.

Describe the first house you remember living in. Take your children on an imaginary tour through the various rooms.

- When you think of that house, what scenes come to mind?
- How old were you when you lived there?
- How old were you when you moved away?
- What was the address?

In our mind's storehouse, many of our memories are filed by the places in which they occurred. Remembering places is a powerful way to unlock the doors of our minds. As you tell your children about a place in your past, often the memories of events and people associated with that place will flow, as if a door has been opened. Out of these places and details, stories may grow.

Tell a story about a time that you remember succeeding and making someone very proud.

- On the flip side, tell a story about something you really dreaded.
- Was it as bad as you'd expected?
- Or did it turn out all right?

Through a story we learned of my parents' following God's call into the ministry—how with four children in tow they moved to another state so that Daddy could go to seminary. Listening to that tale, I learned that my family follows God, wherever he takes them—a lesson most parents want their children to learn and carry with them throughout life.

*Introduce your children
to a childhood friend.*

- Which house did you live in when you knew that friend?
- How old were you, or which grade were you in?
- How and where did you meet that person?
- What games did you play?
- Who else played with the two of you?
- Now introduce us to another friend, from another age or place.

Whenever you tell about an event or a person, it is important to set the story into a specific time and place. If you begin with, "When I was eight years old and we lived in our two-story house in Rome, Georgia," you give the listener a framework for visualizing the setting of the story.

*Describe the first pet
you remember having.*

- What kind of animal was it and what was its name?
- Was it your pet, or did you share it with your brothers and sisters?
- From whom or from where did you get it?
- Tell a story about something that pet did.

*Tell about a time
when you were sick or injured.*

- How old were you and where were you living?
- What was the matter with you?
- Who took care of you?
- Did you see a doctor or go to the hospital?
- Did you miss school?

One of my earliest memories is of having earaches when I was no more than three or four years old. Mother made a pallet near a heater and kept a warm cloth against the ear that hurt. I remember her stroking my forehead gently with her hand.

My Brother's Bike Accident

This story is an example of an on-the-spot anecdote. This type of story arises naturally when something happens that triggers a memory. You then tell your children a story about the memory, on the spot.

This story started one day, when my nieces Brannon and Lillian were visiting. Brannon, age ten, fell while riding her bicycle. As I helped her into the house and washed off her skinned knee, I remembered, for the first time in years, the day her father hurt himself on a bicycle. As I bandaged Brannon's knee, I told her this story:

You know, I saw your daddy have a bicycle accident once. I was probably eight or nine years old, so he must have been twelve or thirteen. We lived in Ellijay, and our house was on the side of a mountain. Your daddy was riding his bike down the hill when he hit a patch of gravel, and he wiped out.

I remember seeing him get up. I must have run down the hill to check on him. He was my big brother, you know. When he stood up, I could see the blood pouring down his face from a cut above his

eye. But he got up saying he was all right—until he touched where it hurt and brought his hand down covered with blood. Then he decided he was hurt.

My mama and daddy—your grandmother and grandfather—took Terry to the doctor, and he got four stitches. If you look at his eyebrow even today, you can see the scar from those stitches.

By the end of the story, I was also done cleaning and bandaging Brannon's knee. Brannon had stopped crying. And I had most of the children in the house as an audience.

Another way to come up with family stories is to listen to some of the experts. Our family has acquired several audio tapes of master storytellers Donald Davis and Kathryn Tucker Windham, both of whom tell family stories. Listening to both of these talented storytellers has given us story ideas and shown us ways to enhance our own accounts of personal experiences.

Several weeks ago I had the privilege of going to hear Donald Davis in person. His marvelous stories of his kindergarten teacher and of his uncle Frank kept the audience in stitches and occasionally brought on tears. On the way home, in a van with seven people, each of us was inspired to tell our own stories.

*Describe your first bedroom
as it was when you were a child.*

- Did you share your room with someone else?
- What did it look like?
- Did the room have wallpaper?
- What colors do you remember in that room?
- What happened in that room?

Often, as we remember stories of our past, we describe only what we saw. But think about the other four senses, too. What smell do you associate with each memory? Which sounds (especially music)? How did someone or something feel to the touch? What tastes or foods do you think of? Sensory details add texture and flavor to your stories.

*Tell the story
of a birthday party
at which you had
a really good time.*

- How old were you?
- In which house did you live?
- Who came to the party?
- What made it so special?
- Now tell a story about that other birthday—the one you wish had never happened.

Photo albums are a wonderful way to jog your memory and illustrate some of your stories. As you reminisce over the photos, your children will love to see pictures of you and your brothers and sisters as children and your parents as young adults.

*Who was your favorite
(or least favorite, or strangest,
or most eccentric) relative?*

Details are important for interest and color. Details add to the child's visual picture. When I tell my children a story about Aunt Mary, I describe the dress she was wearing and the way her hair was fixed. I remind them that her hair was the color of Benjamin's and her eyes were blue like his, too. That description helps them visualize her, even though my three youngest children do not remember ever seeing her.

*Did you have a special
hiding place as a child?
Tell about an adventure there.*

Changing the pace of the story adds interest. If you have prepared notes, find places where the narrative should go faster. Decide where you should talk more slowly. Pause for dramatic effect at suspenseful parts. Any part of your story that lends itself to acting out or verbal emphasis makes the story that much more visual for the listener.

*Tell about a time
you spent the night
away from home.*

- Did you go to camp or were you at a friend's house?
- How old were you?
- What people were there?
- What did you like best about it? Least?
- How did it end?
- Tell about a time when you had friends over to your house.

You can actively involve your children in the story by asking questions. Two or three times during a story, you can stop and ask questions like "Have you ever done anything like this?" or "How do you think I felt?"

*Take an imaginary walk
outside your childhood home.
Tell what you would have seen.*

- Was there a garden?
- Describe the flowers or vegetables growing there.
- Was there a tree you liked to climb?
- What could you see from the top of the tree?
- What games did you play?
- Tell what you would see as you walked through your neighborhood.

I remember my mother's walking us to the library for story time. On the way home we stopped at a bakery and had gingerbread men for a treat. If I close my eyes, I can still smell the delicious aroma inside that bakery. I can still feel my mother's hand holding mine.

Tell about a time when you got lost or separated from your family while away from home.

The use of repetition or refrain creates interest. Repeating key words or phrases establishes a rhythm. But variety in the repetition is also valuable. If, in a story, you describe being lost, next time use the words *gone, missing, disappeared,* or *vanished.*

*Tell the story
of your first day of school.*

- Did your mother or father walk you into school?
- Were you frightened, worried, or excited about going?
- Did you cry, get sick, or misbehave?

*Tell about going to school
on an ordinary morning.*

- Did you walk to school, ride a bus, bike, or ride in a car?
- What did you pass along the way?
- Take your children on an imaginary tour of your school.
- What smells do you remember?
- What colors?
- What other schools did you attend?
- In what towns?
- What was different or special about the schools?

> *Gregg experienced real diversity in his schooling, beginning first grade in a two-room elementary school in rural Michigan and attending third and fourth grade in Oklahoma City in what was the largest consolidated school district in the U.S. at the time. The fourth grade alone occupied two buildings.*

Relate some of your school experiences—favorite grade, a trip to the principal's office, or the funniest thing that ever happened at school.

Iremember listening to my father tell stories about his childhood. On his first day of school Daddy misbehaved so badly that the principal walked him home and informed his mother that he would have to wait another year to come back. I laughed at that story, but I walked away knowing that our family loved our children even when they were rascals, that we looked out for each other but were also expected to do our best, and that we valued education. I learned these values much more effectively through the story than I could have through any lecture.

What do you remember about your favorite teacher both at school and at Sunday school?

- What was his or her name?
- Why did you like this particular teacher?
- Did you ever get into trouble?
- How were you disciplined?
- Do you remember any lessons that were taught?
- Do you still know that teacher?
- Now tell about your least favorite teacher.

> *Repetition jogs our memory, and each time we tell a story we remember another detail to add. Or we think of another way to fill out the story, to make it more dramatic, or to involve our children.*

*Tell about a teacher
who encouraged you.*

- What was his or her name?
- What grade were you in?
- In which school?
- Where did you live?
- Now tell about a teacher who was unfair.
- Tell about good and bad principals.

> *When I was in fifth grade, we moved to Rome, Georgia, and I had to go to a new school. One day when I wore a purple jumper to school, I had to stand up and give a short oral report. The teacher thanked me for my good report and added, "You look so pretty in purple!" I do not remember that teacher's name, but I remember her kindness to me. And purple is still one of my favorite colors.*

*Describe a time
you did poorly in school.*

- What subject did you have trouble with?
- Did you like the teacher?
- How did your parents find out?
- How did they deal with the problem?
- Now think about a time you did well in school.
- What subjects did you like best?
- What special privileges did you have in school? School patrol or crossing guard? Classroom monitor?

> *Tell stories about your failures as well as your successes. When your child gets a bad grade, tell about the "D" you got in sixth grade. If your child strikes out in an important game, tell about the time you let your team down. Let your children hear about your biggest disappointments as well as your proudest moments.*

*Did you ever have a part
in the school play?*

- Did you play in the school band or orchestra?
- Did you ever sing a solo in choir?
- Did you go on any trips with the band or choir? Tell about them.

When I was in second grade, I had the black-cat role in a Halloween play. My costume of black furlike material was so soft to touch. I was disappointed that I had no lines—I was to walk across the stage once during the performance. My mother assured me that the black cat was the most important part. "How could they have a Halloween play without a black cat?" she asked me. And I walked across that stage confident that my part was essential to the show.

*Describe what you
usually did after school.*

Any time can be story time. I tell stories at the obvious times: bedtime, mealtime, on long trips in the car, around the campfire on vacation, and at family gatherings. And I tell stories at other times: when we wait at doctor's offices, or when we wait for Lisette to finish her piano lesson. Anytime we have to wait can be story time.

What was the first big purchase for which you saved your money? Describe both the anticipation and the fulfillment of your plans.

As your children approach their teenage years, be sure to tell them stories of your own struggles as a teen. This not only lets them know what the coming years may hold, but it also reminds you of what to expect. And it will help you empathize with your teen.

Gregg's Baseball Uniforms

One of our family's favorite storytellers, Kathryn Tucker Windham, talks about grits on one of her storytelling tapes. She spends five or six minutes reminiscing about the ways her mother fixed grits when she was a child, the occasions on which she remembers eating grits, and so on. Since we heard that tape, we've begun to classify any such collections of interesting facts, thoughts, and memories on a subjects as a "grits story"—even though the facts may not add up to a true "story."

For example, this past spring when our children's baseball, softball, and T-ball uniforms arrived, they looked at the different styles of each and began to compare them. Gregg then told them about the baseball uniforms he had worn as a child. His reminiscing quickly grew into this grits story:

I remember getting my first baseball uniform when I was eleven years old. I played for a brand-new Little League team called the Giants. In those days, one company didn't sponsor a whole team. A number of businesses would contribute enough for two or three uniforms each. That meant that most of the members of our team had different sponsor names on their shirts.

My shirt had the name "Fitch's IGA" on it.

(The children laughed at that, because they have been to that store on visits to their grandparents.)

And that uniform was made out of a very heavy gray flannel material. So it was hot to wear. But the uniforms lasted for several years. We didn't get new ones each year, like you do now. You just wore whichever one fit best. But we'd proudly wear those uniforms when we marched in the opening-day parade each year.

(At this, the children wanted to know whether or not their dad had played on a winning team.)

The Giants were an expansion team that first year. So none of our players had ever played before. We lost our first pre-season game by the score of 63–1. But I scored the one run for our team, so that made me feel a little better. After that our league enacted a slaughter rule. That's where they end a baseball game when one team gets twenty runs or so ahead.

(The children wanted to know what position their dad had played.)

I played catcher. I was always throwing my mask in the dirt

whenever I had to chase a wild pitch, so I would go home from every ball game with my face muddy and streaked with rivers of sweat. I still remember the gritty feel of my face, the smell of that sweaty mud, and the wonderful taste of the ice cold Coca-Cola we drank after those hot Saturday afternoon games.

Tell about your experience playing sports. Were you ever the hero? When did you let the team down?

- What was the most fun about playing sports?
- What disappointments do you remember?
- Tell about a memorable victory or defeat.
- What do you remember about your coaches?

The more stories children hear, the better listening skills they develop. Their attention span will become longer. And older children enjoy listening again to stories they liked when they were younger. My five children, ages five to fifteen, enjoy the same stories.

*Tell about hobbies you had
while growing up.*

- Did you collect anything?
- Did you build models, do woodworking, sew, do needlework, read, write letters, keep a journal, hike, fish, hunt, or camp?
- How did you get started?
- Who helped or inspired you?
- Where were you living and how old were you at the time?
- How long did you continue that hobby?
- Did you ever encounter trouble in doing something connected with your hobby?

Make eye contact with your children as you tell a story. Eye contact not only draws the audience in, it also keeps the teller in touch with the audience. If you see their interest waning, ask a question to draw them back into the story or bring the story to a close.

*Describe the first church
you remember attending.*

- Take your children on an imaginary trip into the church.
- What music would they hear?
- What would it smell like?
- What would the pews feel like?
- Describe the windows and the pulpit area.
- Tell about attending Vacation Bible School, a church club program, or children's choir.

*Did anything funny or unexpected
ever happen in church?
Tell the story of a time
you acted up in church.*

Singing in Church

My sister Carol and I asked my father to let us sing in church. This was when we lived in Griffin, Georgia, at my father's first full-time pastorate. Carol was six or seven, and I was four or five. We practiced "Jesus Loves Me" over and over and begged Daddy to let us sing it in church. Daddy finally said yes and introduced us in church as the featured music. We hid under the pews. Nothing would get us to come out. The true testimony of my father's love for us was that a month or two later we were asking again, and my father actually introduced us a second time from the pulpit. A second time we hid under the pew! We never again asked to sing in church.

Tell about your family's Christmas traditions.

Story Starter

- What were your family's Christmas traditions?
- What special foods do you associate with Christmas?
- What traditions from the past do you still keep?
- How did your family celebrate other holidays?
- Tell about the family holiday gathering when everything went wrong.

Family gatherings are places to ask questions, learn new family stories, and fill in the details of your own memories. When I see my mother and aunts and uncles, I ask questions. Sometimes I find my memory is sadly inaccurate. I have come to realize, though, that no two people tell the same story about the same event. My mother, my brother, and I each tell the story of the day when my family was on vacation in Kentucky and I was left at a gas station. The three of us laugh and tease each other about which of our versions is the "correct" one, because the three stories are very different!

*What do you remember about your
first encounter with death?*

- Tell the story of the first funeral you remember.
- How old were you?
- In what town did the funeral take place?
- Who had died?
- Who else was there?
- Did the family tell stories about the deceased?
- Did people laugh?
- Were you frightened before the funeral? Sad? Lonely? Puzzled?
- How about afterward?

*Tell about the first wedding
you remember going to.*

- Where was the wedding held?
- How was the church decorated?
- How old were you?
- Who was getting married and how did you know them?
- What family members were also at the wedding?

When I was eight or nine, I attended the wedding of my cousin Gail. We had to drive for a long time to get to the church. My Aunt Veek rode in the car with us, telling us stories and making us laugh. The wedding was in a large Catholic church. We seemed to be miles from the front of the church, and the ceremony seemed to last forever.

What was special about your grandmother or grandfather?

- What memories do you have of your grandparents playing or talking with you?
- What songs did they sing with you?
- What stories did they tell?
- Describe the home your grandparents lived in.

> *My own father used to bathe my children when they were small. At the end of bath time, he would "splish 'em and splash 'em and after a while wash 'em," while he jostled and swirled them around in the tub to rinse them off. My oldest children still remember that silly rhyme.*

Tell a story about a really good time you had visiting your grandparents for a holiday.

- How old were you?
- Describe where the story took place.
- Who else was there?
- What holiday was it?
- What did you do?
- What did your grandparents do?
- Tell about a holiday with your grandparents when something went wrong.

Do not wait until your story is "perfect" to tell it. Most of us stumble around some as we tell a story for the first time. Children are very forgiving audiences.

Do not wait to be a great storyteller, either. According to Sylvia Ziskind, author of Telling Stories to Children, *"Everybody likes to tell a story. Little children do it effortlessly. Great artists do it with native talent and years of practice. Somewhere in between stand you and I."*

*What is the first
(best, worst, or most memorable)
trip you remember taking
with your family?*

- How old were you?
- Where did you go on the trip?
- How did you travel?
- What family members or guests went with you?
- What happened on that trip that was interesting? Disappointing?
- Do you remember something you learned on that trip?
- Who did you visit or meet on the trip?

When I was four years old, my family went to Florida. Mother and Daddy woke us up while it was dark and loaded us into a small trailer that Daddy had made. They had put a mattress into the bottom of the trailer, and we children slept as we traveled. The trailer was covered with a tarp that was only inches above our faces. Sometime the next day, one of the tires on the trailer blew out. I can still remember the smell of burning rubber. When we arrived in Florida, we stayed in a small beach-front cottage and went to the water every day.

*What one traumatic event
from your childhood
stands out in your memory?*

Often when people think of family stories, their first thought is of major traumas: the tornado that knocked the house down, the loss of a mother or father, an automobile accident. Because these events carry such strong emotional impact, they stand out in our memories in clear detail and make powerful family stories.

Recount a "most embarrassing moment" from your childhood.

Our friend Robert grew up in a sadly dysfunctional family, yet he told his children the stories of his childhood that included his football coach, a warm Christian man who encouraged Robert when his father wouldn't. Robert's children, now grown with children of their own, learned that God is present even in difficult circumstances, that with God's help people can overcome problems, and that compassion is important. And Robert, in telling those stories, remembered warm moments with his parents. Even though they seemed unable to rise above their personal problems, they loved their son and were sometimes able to show that love. The stories remind Robert of the good times and let him put the bad times into perspective and find emotional healing. Robert's mother now lives with him and his wife. His family, knowing the stories of his youth, see the power of forgiveness in their father's life.

Recall some big plans you had that didn't turn out at all like you expected.

One nice thing about a book of questions like this is that you can use it again and again with different results. A quick one-time read-through may trigger one layer of especially memorable details and stories. If you read through the book again a month from now, or talk through the questions with a family member, your mind will make some new connections. And if you really take some time and pick just two or three questions to focus your brainstorming on, you'll often uncover additional levels of details and experiences long buried in the marvelous stockpile of your memories.

These questions are merely a starting point, a sampling of possible memory prods. You may want to come up with other questions of your own, because there's so much you could tell and so much your children would like to know about when their parents were children.

Tell a story about a time your guardian angel must have been watching over you.

Sometimes I end a story by asking, "Who lived at my house then?" and we review the names of my brothers and sisters, giving my children a picture of my original family. They always think it's funny that Uncle Terry was a little boy and was my brother, and they were amazed when they found out that their father did not grow up with my family.

When I was two months old, I almost died of pneumonia. I told my children the story of my illness several times before I thought of a good ending. Now, at that story's end, we list the people whom we love who would not be alive today if God had not answered prayers and made me well.

However you decide to conclude a story, your conclusion should be brief and to the point, without a long moral or a complicated interpretation. The listeners should be able to draw their own conclusions. The next time they hear the story, they may find an entirely different lesson to be learned.

"Did I Ever Tell You About . . ."

The more stories you tell, the more stories you will remember. Usually one story will remind you of another. Or, a story will come to mind from something your child says or does, or from a situation that you or someone in your family faces today.

One day my children and I witnessed an automobile accident. While we waited for the cars to be moved, I told them about the first wreck I witnessed as a child. I was with my father when we came upon a small sports car that had collided with an eighteen-wheeler. The people in other cars just sat and watched, but my father got out and went to see if he could help. One of the two girls in the sports car was unconscious, the other awake but badly injured. Daddy prayed aloud for the girls, until the first girl also lost consciousness. Neither girl lived, but at least someone was praying for them as they died.

On the day I told my children that story, the police and ambulance came quickly. At the end of the story, we prayed for the people in the wrecked cars ahead of us. Since that day, when we've seen an accident or heard a siren, my children suggest that we pray for the people involved.

Remember to tell the stories of how God has worked in your life. Several months ago, twelve-year-old Matthew and I left early one Saturday morning to shop at yard sales. We were looking primarily for toys for our church nursery. We also knew that the Sunday school desperately needed a piece of climbing equipment for a group of active four- and five-year-old boys. As we drove away from the house, Matthew and I prayed that God would help us find the yard sales with toys. "And, Lord," I added, "We would love to find a climber for that four-year-old room!" God answered with a resounding "Yes!" Every yard sale we found had toys or books that we wanted. At the last one, we found a $300 wood climber for $20!

Do not neglect to tell stories that are hard to tell. Stories of sadness and hardship give children a new perspective. They see how someone else faced troubles and triumphed, lived through sadness and found happiness again. And don't forget to tell stories about

your mistakes, your weaknesses, and your failures. These can teach children what it means to be human. They enable our listeners to really know us and at the same time allow us to feel truly known and loved—a big part of what belonging to a family is all about.

When we once again tell our children family stories, we can rediscover a powerful means of communicating with the next generation. Stories reach past our minds and into our hearts. They bring us into the situation, make us empathize and identify with the characters, reinforce our sense of family identity, bolster our self-esteem, and define our personal and family values. Stories bridge the gap between listener and teller, as people throughout the centuries have known, and as Jesus demonstrated through the telling of many parables. Stories are a good place to express feelings, to share or test ideas, to gain new knowledge, and to pass on values.

Family storytelling is more than just an effective means of communicating family values. It is a gift you give your children. Each time you tell a family story, you have not only given them your time and attention but also a piece of yourself. And your children can pass that gift on to their children.

We trust that as you have read, you have begun experimenting with family storytelling—recounting those stories that define your family as uniquely your own. We hope you have been having fun, because family storytelling should be enjoyable for all.

As you tell family stories to your children, it will become a habit, woven into the very fabric of your relationships. Storytelling will become easier as you practice. Your children will think to ask for family stories more often, and you'll find yourself regularly asking, "Did I ever tell you about . . . ?"

Enter the Creating Family Memories Contest!

Do you have a family story to share? It could get you published! Or send you on a family vacation of a lifetime!

Here's How. Write out your favorite family story and mail it to the address below. Your story will be judged on its originality and on how well the event created a lasting memory or drew your family together. The story must be original and not previously published, typed or neatly handwritten, and 500 words or less.

The Prizes. The ten best stories will be published in *Christian Parenting* ($100 value). Grand prize is a six-day, five-night family vacation for four to anywhere in the continental United States. The contest is cosponsored by USAir and Holiday Inn.

Mail in your story with your name, address, and phone number to: Creating Family Memories, Attn. Betty Wood B16, Zondervan Publishing House, Grand Rapids, MI 49530.

The Official Rules. No purchase necessary. Ten winners will be published in *Christian Parenting* magazine ($100 value). One grand prize consists of six days, five nights at a Holiday Inn, round-trip airfare on USAir, rental car, and $200 spending money, for a total $2,500 value. No cash substitute. Entries must be received by March 31, 1995. Judging will be conducted by a panel, and its decisions shall be final. Sponsor not responsible for lost or damaged mail. Taxes are winners' responsibility. All entries become the property of sponsor. The contest is open to residents of the United States, 21 years and older. All prizes will be awarded. Employees or their family members of Zondervan, Family Bookstores, HarperCollins, or their advertising affiliates may not enter. A list of prize winners may be obtained after July 31, 1995 by sending a self-addressed, stamped envelope to the address listed above.